CURIOSITY

Shannon Welbourn

www.av2books.com

Step 1
Go to www.av2books.com

Step 2
Enter this unique code

VWSNINT5Y

Step 3
Explore your interactive eBook!

AV2 is optimized for use on any device

Your interactive eBook comes with...

Contents
Browse a live contents page to easily navigate through resources

Audio
Listen to sections of the book read aloud

Videos
Watch informative video clips

Weblinks
Gain additional information for research

Try This!
Complete activities and hands-on experiments

Key Words
Study vocabulary, and complete a matching word activity

Quizzes
Test your knowledge

Slideshows
View images and captions

... and much, much more!

CURIOSITY

Contents

4	What Is Curiosity?
6	Why Is Curiosity Important?
8	Biography: Clara Ma
10	Curiosity at Home
12	Curiosity at School
14	Curiosity in Your Community
16	Case Study: Rotary Club Exchange
18	Overcoming Challenges
20	Encouraging Curiosity in Others
22	Curiosity in Action
23	Key Words/Index

What Is Curiosity?

Why is Earth called the Blue Planet? How do we know what dinosaurs looked like? When people are curious, they ask questions to learn about things that interest them.

Curiosity is the **desire** to learn or know something. People who are curious are excited to **explore** and learn new things. They ask questions and work to find answers. What kinds of things do you have questions about? Curiosity drives you to develop a deeper understanding about things that interest you.

When you ask questions, you start to explore new ideas. Each new question you ask helps you learn things you did not know before. Answers can lead to new questions and ideas. Curiosity helps you develop an active mind, which means that you are constantly thinking and questioning.

Curiosity can lead you in new directions. This girl is curious about how plants grow. She works to explore answers!

Be Your Best

Everyone has curiosity. Just like a muscle in your body, you need to use it to keep it strong.

Curiosity   **5**

Why is Curiosity Important?

Curiosity is important because it opens your mind to learning about the world and discovering new things.

Curiosity has helped shape our world. Think about all of the amazing inventions around the world. These creations or discoveries would not have happened without curious minds. What would our world be like if Thomas Edison had not been not curious about **electric** light? What if Alexander Graham Bell and others had not been curious about communications through telephone lines?

Curiosity can lead to **innovations**. A curious mind came up with the idea to use robots in factories to make work easier.

When a curious person sees a problem to solve, they start asking questions. They look beyond what is already known and search to understand more. They look for possibilities to create or improve things. With curiosity, learning becomes an exciting journey of discovery!

BIOGRAPHY

Clara Ma

Following your curiosity leads you to topics and activities that interest you.

Clara Ma was always fascinated with stars, planets, and space. Clara's grandma helped her curiosity grow by talking to her about **constellations** of stars in the night sky. Clara was also curious about what might exist in the universe beyond the stars. One day in science class, she learned about an essay competition to name the **Mars Rover**, a robot that was being sent to space to explore Mars. She thought of her own curiosity about space and felt the rover represented others' curiosity about space, too. Her essay suggested naming the rover "Curiosity." Her idea won!

NAME: Clara Ma
FROM: Prairie Village, Kansas
ACCOMPLISHMENT: Winner of the Mars Science Laboratory essay competition

"Curiosity is the **passion** that drives us through our everyday lives. We have become explorers and scientists with our need to ask questions and wonder."
—Clara Ma, from her winning essay

Be Your Best

Clara Ma was just 12 years old when she won the competition to name the Mars Rover.

Mars is the **fourth** planet in the Solar System. A year on Mars lasts **687** days.

Curiosity launched on November 26, 2011. It landed on Mars **253** days later, in August 2012.

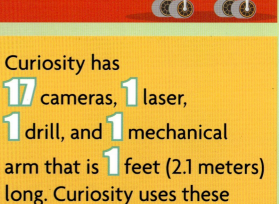

Curiosity has **17** cameras, **1** laser, **1** drill, and **1** mechanical arm that is **1** feet (2.1 meters) long. Curiosity uses these tools to study rocks.

Curiosity 9

Curiosity at Home

Your home is the first place that your curiosity grows.

At a young age, you explore and learn new sights and sounds. As you get older, you can develop your curiosity by watching and learning from your family members. Curious people value what others can teach them.

Maybe your dad makes amazing cookies and you are curious to know how he does it.

Curious people know they can learn from others around them.

Learn to Make Decisions

Think of a question you could ask to learn something new about a family member.

You can build your curiosity by asking questions and learning about your family members. What was life like for them when they were your age? Your parents, grandparents, or caregivers all have their own interesting stories to tell. Ask questions! Pay attention and listen closely to the stories they share.

Curiosity at School

While you are at school, you are constantly learning new things. People who are curious enjoy learning and exploring new ideas.

You can grow your curiosity by showing that you are excited to learn. Do not be afraid to ask questions when you do not understand. There is nothing wrong with saying you do not know the answer. Asking questions and finding answers builds curiosity.

When your curiosity grows, you learn more. Let your interests drive you, and never stop on your path to learning!

Learn to Make Decisions

What is something you have been interested to learn more about? How can you explore the topic to learn more about it?

Curious people are active learners. They do not wait for someone to give them answers. They take action to find out things for themselves. New learning often begins by asking "what," "why," "where," "when," "who," and "how." Finding answers to these questions gives us a basic understanding of something. To dig deeper, curious people ask questions such as, "What would happen if…?" and "How do we know…?"

If you were curious about how polar bears survive in the Arctic, you might ask questions such as, "What do polar bears eat?" or "What would happen if the Arctic got warmer?"

Curiosity in Your Community

A community is a group of people who live, work, and play in a place. Your home, school, and neighborhood are part of your community.

Being curious about how the world works is the first step in discovering ways to improve it. The world is a huge place, and we can start by being curious in our communities.

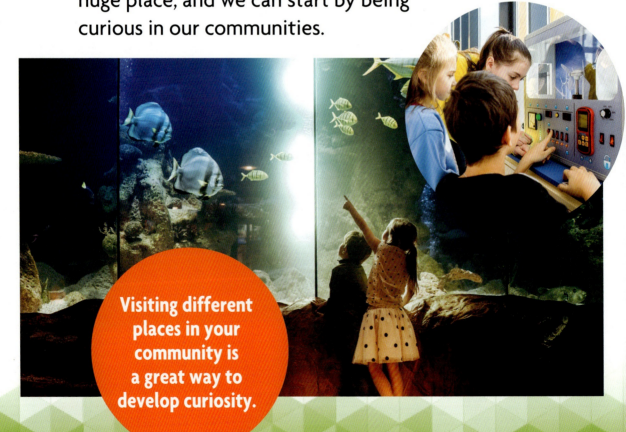

Visiting different places in your community is a great way to develop curiosity.

Curious people are open to new experiences. This means they are willing to learn and try new things. Sometimes you may not even know you are interested in something until you spend some time learning about it. Many libraries and community centers offer free clubs or classes for kids to join. Ask an adult to help you learn what programs are available in your community. From hiking on local nature trails to visiting a nearby farm, each new experience is a chance to discover and grow. You may be surprised by what you learn and might develop a strong interest to explore further.

CASE STUDY

Rotary Club Exchange

Do you ever wonder how people in other parts of the world live? Curious people are often interested in people, places, and things beyond their own communities. This curiosity helps people better understand how we are all connected.

Some organizations have programs that give young people a chance to travel to other countries and learn about different ways of life. For example, the Rotary Club is a community group that offers a youth exchange program. The program provides young people with a chance to live in another country for up to one year.

NAME: Rotary Club Exchange
FROM: Around the world
ACCOMPLISHMENT: Offers programs for youth to explore their curiosity by visiting new places

Be Your Best

Some exchange students may learn a new language. This student is learning to read and write in Chinese.

Students in the program live with host families and attend school. They learn about and experience a new **culture**, or way of life. Exchange students also teach others about their own culture and share what life is like where they live.

Learn to Make Decisions

Are you curious about a certain country or part of the world? What country would you want to visit if you took part in a youth exchange program?

There are more than **35,000** Rotary Clubs around the world.

There are about **7.7 billion** people on Earth.

People around the world speak more than **7,100** different languages.

Curiosity 17

Overcoming Challenges

Challenges can get in the way of our curiosity. A challenge is something that is difficult to achieve, such as finding answers to difficult questions. Sometimes there are no easy answers to our questions, and it can be challenging to keep our curious minds going.

We wonder, and develop many questions, about the world around us. Sometimes, our questions are easy to answer. Some may be more difficult to explore. It is okay to admit that you do not know something. When you do, you allow yourself to think of the next steps to come up with an answer, such as asking others for help or finding a new **resource** for information.

The journey, or **process**, of learning and discovery matters more than finding the right answers. By being curious, you will keep learning and discovering new things throughout your life. Let your curiosity guide you on a journey of lifelong learning!

It can be a challenge to be curious about something that you cannot explore in person, such as outer space. Overcome this challenge by finding other resources to learn from, such as books, the internet, or other people.

Encouraging Curiosity in Others

Each person's curiosity develops in different ways. Something you find interesting may not be of interest to someone else.

We cannot tell others what they should be curious about, but we can show others our excitement for learning new things. You can encourage others' curiosity by helping them explore their interests.

Curious people teach others and are open to learning from others, too.

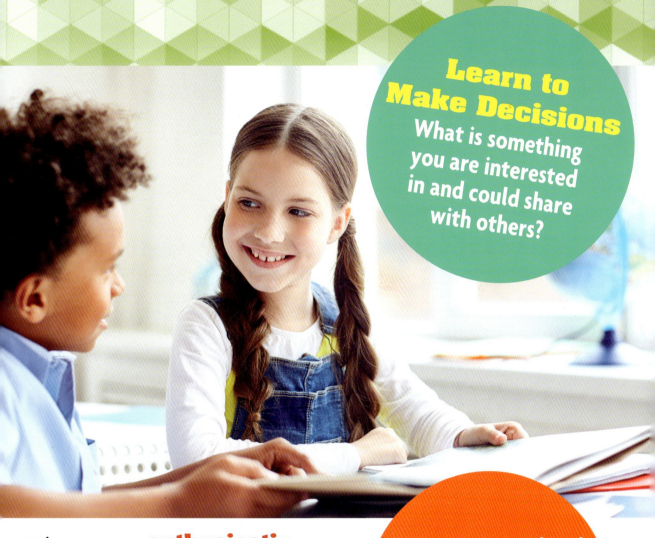

Learn to Make Decisions

What is something you are interested in and could share with others?

When we are **enthusiastic** about a topic, our excitement may lead others to develop an interest. Sharing your love of learning could encourage them to explore something they find interesting. You may also discover ways to **collaborate** with others. Each person may be curious about different things, but when you put their ideas together, everyone's mind grows.

Your curiosity combined with your friend's interest could help you learn and create in new and exciting ways.

Curiosity 21

Curiosity in Action

Take Action! You can learn more about topics that interest you by reading books, visiting websites, talking to people, going on field trips, or trying out something for yourself. Remember: You can never know all there is to know about something!

Use the ideas and tips below to help you grow your curiosity!

Start a Question Journal:

Create a notebook to record your questions. Try to write in it each night before you go to bed. Your questions could come from something that happened during the day, a new thing you noticed, something you saw on television, or anything else. Write down your questions so that you can go back and explore them when you can. Here are some journal question starters to get you started:

- What would happen if…?
- How can I solve the problem?
- What is the best way to…?
- How does it work?

Key Words

collaborate: to work together with others
constellations: groups of stars seen in patterns
culture: the shared beliefs and traditions in a place
desire: the longing for something that brings enjoyment, such as learning
electric: describing something powered by electricity
enthusiastic: full of interest and excitement

explore: to investigate or learn about something
innovations: something new or different that is introduced
Mars Rover: a robotic machine sent by the National Aeronautics and Space Administration (NASA) in the United States to explore Mars
passion: a strong enthusiasm or desire
process: a set of steps or actions followed to achieve something
resource: supply or support needed to do something

Index

community 14, 15, 16

explore 4, 8, 10, 12, 13, 15, 16, 18, 19, 20, 21, 22

home 10, 14

journey 7, 19

Ma, Clara 8, 9
Mars Rover 8, 9

questions 4, 7, 8, 11, 12, 13, 18, 22

Rotary Club Exchange 16, 17

school 12, 14, 17

Get the best of both worlds.

AV2 bridges the gap between print and digital.

The expandable resources toolbar enables quick access to content including **videos**, **audio**, **activities**, **weblinks**, **slideshows**, **quizzes**, and **key words**.

Animated videos make static images come alive.

Resource icons on each page help readers to further **explore key concepts**.

Published by AV2
350 5th Avenue, 59th Floor
New York, NY 10118
Website: www.av2books.com

Copyright ©2021 AV2
All rights reserved. No part of this publication may be reproduced, stored in a retrieval system, or transmitted in any form or by any means, electronic, mechanical, photocopying, recording, or otherwise, without the prior written permission of the publisher.

Library of Congress Control Number: 2020937060

ISBN 978-1-7911-3166-1 (Hardcover)
ISBN 978-1-7911-3167-8 (Softcover)
ISBN 978-1-7911-3168-5 (Multi-user eBook)
ISBN 978-1-7911-3169-2 (Single-user eBook)

Printed in Guangzhou, China
1 2 3 4 5 6 7 8 9 0   24 23 22 21 20

042020
101119

Project Coordinator: Sara Cucini   Designer: Jean Faye Marie Rodriguez

Every reasonable effort has been made to trace ownership and to obtain permission to reprint copyright material. The publishers would be pleased to have any errors or omissions brought to their attention so that they may be corrected in subsequent printings.

The publisher acknowledges Getty Images, iStock, Shutterstock, and the National Aeronautics and Space Administration as its primary image suppliers for this title.

First published by Crabtree Publishing Company in 2017.

View new titles and product videos at www.av2books.com